Utah

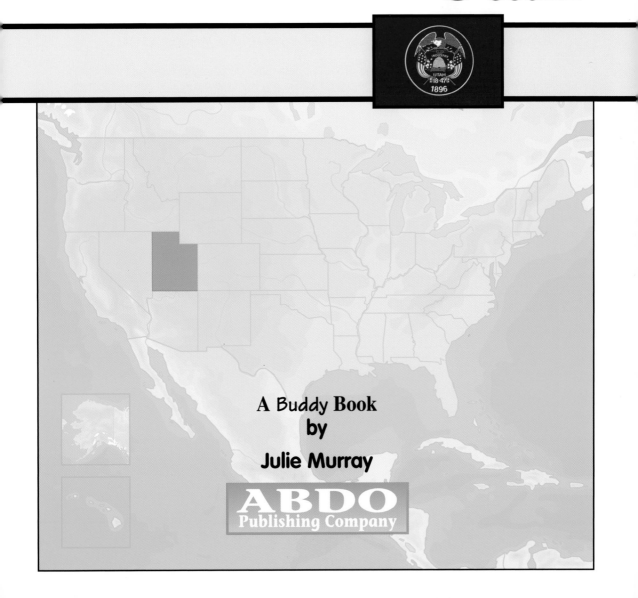

A Buddy Book
by
Julie Murray

ABDO
Publishing Company

VISIT US AT
www.abdopub.com

Published by ABDO Publishing Company, 4940 Viking Drive, Edina, Minnesota 55435.

Copyright © 2006 by Abdo Consulting Group, Inc. International copyrights reserved in all countries. No part of this book may be reproduced in any form without written permission from the publisher. Buddy Books™ is a trademark and logo of ABDO Publishing Company.

Printed in the United States.

Edited by: Sarah Tieck
Contributing Editor: Michael P. Goecke
Graphic Design: Deb Coldiron, Maria Hosley
Image Research: Sarah Tieck
Photographs: AP/Wide World, Clipart.com, Digital Vision, Eyewire, Getty Images, Library of Congress, One Mile Up, Photodisc, Photos.com, Super Stock

Library of Congress Cataloging-in-Publication Data

Murray, Julie, 1969-
    Utah / Julie Murray.
        p. cm. — (The United States)
    Includes index.
    ISBN 1-59197-703-7
        1. Utah—Juvenile literature. I. Title.

F826.3.M87 2006
979.2—dc22

                                                                    2005049026

Table Of Contents

A Snapshot Of Utah

Utah is known as the home of the Great Salt Lake. This is the largest saltwater lake in the United States. Utah also has mountains, valleys, rivers, and unique rock formations.

There are 50 states in the United States. Every state is different. Every state has an official nickname. Utah's nickname is the "Beehive State." This comes from a Mormon word that means "honey bee." This is because of the hard work it takes to survive in this area.

Utah became the 45th state on January 4, 1896. It is the 11th-largest state in the United States. It has 84,905 square miles (219,903 sq km) of land. It is home to 2,233,169 people.

There are many rivers and natural areas in Utah's landscape.

Where Is Utah?

There are four parts of the United States. Each part is called a region. Each region is in a different area of the country. The United States Census Bureau says the four regions are the Northeast, the South, the Midwest, and the West.

Utah is located in the West region of the United States. Utah's weather is mild and sunny in the summer months. It is cold in the winter months. Sometimes it snows in some of Utah's mountains.

Four Regions of the United States of America

ALASKA

WASHINGTON
MONTANA
NORTH DAKOTA
MINNESOTA
VERMONT
MAINE
OREGON
IDAHO
SOUTH DAKOTA
WISCONSIN
MICHIGAN
NEW YORK
NEW HAMPSHIRE
MASSACHUSETTS
WYOMING
IOWA
PENNSYLVANIA
RHODE ISLAND
CONNECTICUT
NEVADA
NEBRASKA
OHIO
NEW JERSEY
DELAWARE
UTAH
COLORADO
ILLINOIS
INDIANA
WEST VIRGINIA
VIRGINIA
Washington D.C.
MARYLAND
CALIFORNIA
KANSAS
MISSOURI
KENTUCKY
OKLAHOMA
ARKANSAS
TENNESSEE
NORTH CAROLINA
ARIZONA
NEW MEXICO
MISSISSIPPI
ALABAMA
GEORGIA
SOUTH CAROLINA
TEXAS
LOUISIANA
FLORIDA

HAWAII

	West		Midwest		South		Northeast

Utah has warm and sunny weather during the summer months.

Utah shares its borders with six other states. Idaho is north. Wyoming is northeast. Colorado is east. Arizona is south. Nevada is west. And, New Mexico touches the southeast corner of Utah.

Utah is part of the Four Corners. This is where New Mexico, Arizona, Utah, and Colorado all meet. It is the only location in the United States where four states meet.

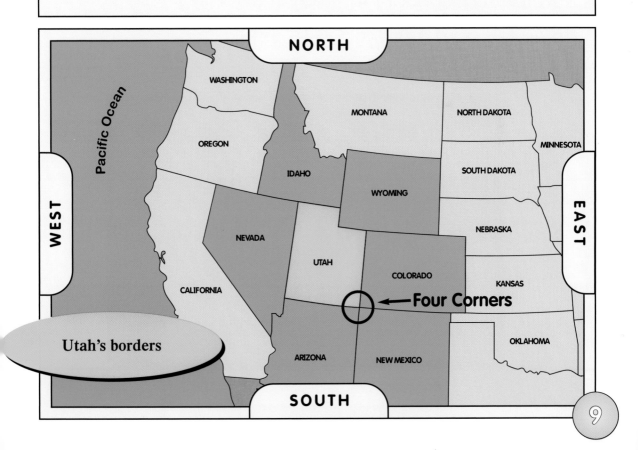

Utah

State abbreviation: **UT**

State nickname: Beehive State

State capital: Salt Lake City

State motto: Industry

Statehood: January 4, 1896, 45th state

Population: 2,233,169, ranks 34th

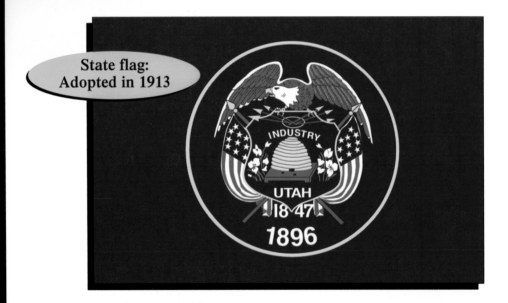

State flag:
Adopted in 1913

Land area: 84,905 square miles (219,903 sq km), ranks 11th

State tree: Blue spruce

State song: "Utah, We Love Thee"

State government: Three branches: legislative, executive, and judicial

Average July temperature: 73°F (23°C)

Average January temperature: 25°F (-4°C)

State bird:
Seagull

State animal:
Elk

State flower:
Sego lily

Cities And The Capital

Salt Lake City is the capital of Utah. It is also the state's largest city. Salt Lake City is located in the north central part of the state. Temple Square is in downtown Salt Lake City. The Mormon Tabernacle is nearby. That is where the famous Mormon Tabernacle Choir performs.

A view of Salt Lake City.

The Capitol of Utah.

Ogden is one of the largest cities in Utah. It is north of Salt Lake City. The two cities are part of a large metropolitan area. There are 1,333,914 people living in this metropolitan area.

Famous Citizens

Brigham Young (1801–1877)

Brigham Young was born in 1801. He was a very important person in Utah and the American West. He was the president of The Church of Jesus Christ of Latter-day Saints. This is also called the Mormon Church. He helped build the church. He also founded many towns and cities. He encouraged people to move west. Brigham Young University in Salt Lake City is named after him.

Brigham Young

Famous Citizens

Donny Osmond (1957–)

Donny Osmond was born in 1957 in Ogden. He and his sister, Marie, became famous singers in the 1970s. They starred in the *Donny and Marie* show on television. Later, Osmond went on to perform in musicals. One of the most popular was Andrew Lloyd Webber's *Joseph and the Amazing Technicolor Dreamcoat*.

Donny Osmond

The Mormons

The Mormons are said to be Utah's first settlers. About 150 Mormons arrived there in 1847. At that time, Utah was a great wilderness.

Mormon pioneers in 1847.

The Mormon people had lived in many other parts of the United States before moving to Utah. They wanted a place where they could practice their religion freely. This is because they were often treated badly for their beliefs.

Mormon leader Brigham Young and the Mormon settlers founded Salt Lake City. They also set up their church. This church is now called The Church of Jesus Christ of Latter-day Saints.

The Mormon Tabernacle

Over the years, they played a big role in developing Utah. Today, the Mormon Church has more than 12 million members all over the world. Many Mormons still live in Utah. Salt Lake City is where they have their main church.

The Mormon Temple is in Salt Lake City.

National Parks Of Utah

Utah's national parks are in the southern part of the state. These parks have high cliffs, unique rock formations, and deep canyons.

Bryce Canyon National Park

The landscape of Bryce Canyon is famous.

Bryce Canyon National Park is one of Utah's national parks. It is in southern Utah. Bryce Canyon National Park has cliffs and canyons. It is known for being full of colored rocks. These rocks have formed unusual shapes.

Bryce Canyon's landscape
is rocky and colorful.

Arches National Park is in the southeastern part of Utah. It is located near Moab. It is known for its unusual rock formations, too.

Double Arch is in Arches National Park.

Delicate Arch is another arch at
Arches National Park.

There are thousands of red rocks shaped like arches in the park. Landscape Arch is one of the most famous arches there. It is also one of the longest in the world. It measures 291 feet (89 m).

The Great Salt Lake

The Great Salt Lake is located in the northwestern part of Utah. It is the largest saltwater lake in the United States.

The Great Salt Lake is one of the saltiest bodies of water in the world. It is even saltier than the ocean. The salt in the lake makes floating on the water easy. Also, salt from the Great Salt Lake is used for softening water and for melting ice and snow.

The Great Salt Lake used to be part of Lake Bonneville. Lake Bonneville was a large freshwater lake. Thousands of years ago, there was a flood. The flood changed Lake Bonneville into several smaller lakes. One was the Great Salt Lake.

Today, the Great Salt Lake is about 75 miles (121 km) long and 35 miles (56 km) wide. It changes size with the weather.

A view of the Great Salt Lake.

Utah

1765: Spanish explorer Juan Maria de Rivera arrives in Utah.

1824: Jim Bridger sees the Great Salt Lake. Many believe he is the first European to do this.

1847: Brigham Young and the Mormon pioneers arrive in Utah. They will create Salt Lake City.

A reenactment of the Mormon pioneers' trip to Utah.

1848: The United States gains Utah from Mexico.

1849: Mormons establish the State of Deseret.

1850: The Utah Territory is created. Brigham Young is named governor.

1896: Utah becomes the 45th state on January 4.

1919: Zion National Park is established.

1952: Uranium is found near Moab.

2002: Salt Lake City hosts the 2002 Winter Olympics.

2003: Lieutenant Governor Olene Walker takes over for Governor Michael O. Leavitt. She is the first female governor of Utah.

Cities In Utah

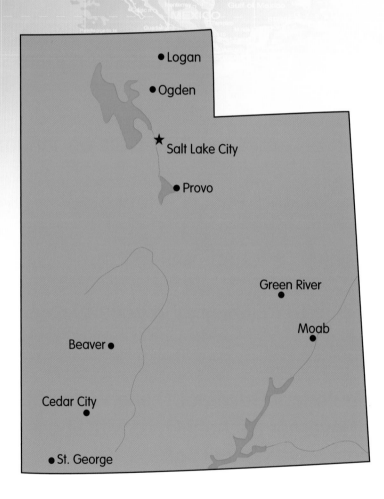

- Logan
- Ogden
- ★ Salt Lake City
- Provo
- Green River
- Moab
- Beaver
- Cedar City
- St. George

Important Words

capital a city where government leaders meet.

metropolitan a large city, usually with smaller communities called suburbs.

Mormon a religious group started by Joseph Smith in 1830 in Fayette, New York.

nickname a name that describes something special about a person or a place.

pioneers people who traveled across the United States in the 1800s to settle the western United States.

tabernacle a large place of worship.

wilderness wild, unsettled land.

Web Sites

To learn more about Utah, visit ABDO Publishing Company on the World Wide Web. Web site links about Utah are featured on our Book Links page. These links are routinely monitored and updated to provide the most current information available.

www.abdopub.com

Index